SOMETIMES I NEVER SUFFERED

SHANE MCCRAE

FARRAR STRAUS GIROUX / NEW YORK

SOMETIMES I NEVER SUFFERED

Farrar, Straus and Giroux
120 Broadway, New York 10271

Library of Congress Cataloging-in-Publication Data
Names: McCrae, Shane, 1975– author.
Title: Sometimes I never suffered / Shane McCrae.
Description: First edition. | New York : Farrar, Straus and Giroux, 2020. |
    Summary: "Spanning religious, historical, and political themes, a new
    collection from the award-winning poet"— Provided by publisher.
Identifiers: LCCN 2020003402 | ISBN 9780374240813 (hardcover)
Subjects: LCGFT: Poetry.
Classification: LCC PS3613.C385747 S66 2020 | DDC 811/.6—dc23
LC record available at https://lccn.loc.gov/2020003402

Our books may be purchased in bulk for promotional, educational, or
business use. Please contact your local bookseller or the Macmillan Corporate
and Premium Sales Department at 1-800-221-7945, extension 5442,
or by e-mail at MacmillanSpecialMarkets@macmillan.com.

www.fsgbooks.com
www.twitter.com/fsgbooks
www.facebook.com/fsgbooks

1 3 5 7 9 10 8 6 4 2

And that's my night sky, before me,
and I'm the child standing under it,
my back getting cold, an ache in my eyes,
and the wall-battering heaven battering me.

OSIP MANDELSTAM

(translated by Clarence Brown
and W. S. Merwin)

CONTENTS

Preface

xiii

Jim Limber in Heaven Is a Nexus at Which the
Many Heavens of the Multiverse Converge

3

I. FRESH EYES FOR A FRESH WORLD

The Hastily Assembled Angel Falls at the Beginning of the World

7

The Wings of the Hastily Assembled Angel

10

The Hastily Assembled Angel Considers
What It Means to Be Made in the Image Of

11

The Hastily Assembled Angel Also Sustains the World

14

The Hastily Assembled Angel on Care and Vitality

17

The Hastily Assembled Angel Considers His Own Foreknowing

18

The Hastily Assembled Angel Meets the God of Human Freedom

20

The Hastily Assembled Angel at the Gate

22

The Tree of Knowledge

23

The Loneliness of the Hastily Assembled Angel

25

The Hastily Assembled Angel Considers the Duties Owed to Love

27

The Hastily Assembled Angel Considers the Lives of Dogs and of People

29

2. VARIATIONS ON JIM LIMBER GOES TO HEAVEN

Jim Limber Tells the Truth About His Fate

33

Jim Limber's Home Is No Earthly Home

34

Jim Limber Describes His Arrival in Heaven

35

Jim Limber Refuses to Enter Heaven Until He Has Lived a Happy Life

36

Jim Limber Enters the Joint Economy of Heaven and Earth

37

Jim Limber on the Inability of the Enslaved to See Themselves

38

Jim Limber's Theodicy

39

Jim Limber on the Ever-Growing Hunger for the New

40

Jim Limber Sees People Get the Heaven They Want

41

Jim Limber on the White Embrace

42

Old Times There

43

LIMBO

Jim Limber Burning Where No Fire Is

55

2. VARIATIONS ON JIM LIMBER GOES TO HEAVEN

Jim Limber on the Gates of Heaven

59

Jim Limber on the Peace Which Passeth All Understanding

60

Jesus and the Mongrel Dog

61

Jim Limber on the Heavenly Reward

65

Jim Limber in Heaven Writes His Name in Water

66

Heaven in Heaven

67

Jim Limber on the Gardens of the Face of God

68

Jim Limber on Continuity in Heaven

69

Jim Limber Tells What He Knows About Heaven

70

Jim Limber on Possibility

71

I. FRESH EYES FOR A FRESH WORLD

The Ladder to Heaven

75

Acknowledgments

85

Sometimes I Never Suffered concludes "A Fire in Every World," a poem begun with "Purgatory/A Son and a Father of Sons" from *In the Language of My Captor*, and continued with "The Hell Poem" from *The Gilded Auction Block*. The whole of *Sometimes I Never Suffered* is the third part of this poem, but, as is the case with the other two parts, it can also be read on its own.

SOMETIMES I NEVER SUFFERED

JIM LIMBER IN HEAVEN IS A NEXUS

AT WHICH THE MANY HEAVENS

OF THE MULTIVERSE CONVERGE

I've been a long time dead without my life
And when it comes   back it comes back to me
In parts and sometimes   I get two or three
Or I don't know how many fif-

teen forty of the same   part like I lived
The same life sixty different ways I'll   see
My face and it's my same face   and I'll be
Standing where I remember standing once   and if

Other folks were there they're there or some
Of them or all   of them but me and some or all of them
Are wearing different outfits like the weath-

er in us changed   I think now more than half
Of life is death   but I can't die
Enough for all the life I see

I. FRESH EYES FOR A FRESH WORLD

Except most things weren't clouds   everything there
Was clouds   the hastily assembled angel
Before he knew the word   *clouds* was the last word
He heard the other angels shouting as
They shoved him   though he after he had fallen
Too far to hear them he   saw their mouths making
Shapes that were not *clouds*   and when he saw that
Thought *That's   something that isn't clouds that   shouting
After I've fallen too far to hear them don't
They know   I've fallen too far to hear them now
Or are we not together now* before
He knew the word   in those few minutes the other
Angels were assembling him   he named
The things he saw with words that seemed to fit them
Nothing was *heavenly* a few things were
Ocean and *hole* and *monkeyapple* he
Before the other angels shoved him   had
Started combining words   but nobody
Would name the things he saw the way he named them
And to the other angels all his naming
Was noise they shouted   as they shoved him *It's*

All   *clouds* what difference could it make   to the angel
Built to monitor the Earth   from the surface
Of the Earth   what was or wasn't true in Heaven
They shoved him then   they stared and then they shouted
After the disappearing figure all
The things they suddenly remembered   they had
Forgotten to tell him   as they were hammer-
ing him together   as they hammered him to-
gether   behind them   but above behind a
Pinkish   amorphous light that was or was-
n't God had pulsed   like the heart of one of the creatures
God hadn't yet created though the angels
Had seen the creatures coming in the waves
Then covering the Earth   the angels had
Seen them   and hadn't wanted   to be forced
To live with them   and so had voted to
Build their own angel but they hadn't asked
Permission first instead they all together
Threw him together   and as Gabriel
Asked God if this new angel   could be sent
Instead to Earth fresh   eyes for a fresh World
The other angels shoved the thrown-   together angel
From the clouds and Heaven   the hastily
Assembled angel   could see farther than
The other angels though he couldn't under-
stand what he saw as well   as the other angels
Would have   and as he fell he saw their mouths

Making shapes he saw the light behind them
Pulsing   and as he fell he watched the clouds
Becoming strange   abstract   the way another
Angel would watch a species go extinct
Even as dry land emerged from the waves below him

THE WINGS OF THE

HASTILY ASSEMBLED ANGEL

The hastily assembled angel flies

With patchwork wings red patches and white patches

And yellow patches blood and emptiness

And sun and usually   an angel's wings would

Be made of only one of these   but his

Were made at the last minute and were almost

Not made at all and wouldn't have been made

Had Azrael not seen   in the hastily

Assembled angel's eyes   as Azrael

Placed his   white palm on the hastily assembled

Angel's chest   fear   as Azrael placed his palm there

To shove him from the cloud   and saw he had

No wings   and paused and thought   then pulled him back

And so the angels stitched together what was

Near   blood   emptiness   sun   since what was near

Was Heaven   and what else would Heaven be

THE HASTILY ASSEMBLED ANGEL CONSIDERS

WHAT IT MEANS TO BE MADE IN THE IMAGE OF

Humans being made   in the image not of God
Directly but of the angel   who the day God made
Human beings most resembled God   who changes
The way light changes as the sun in the morning

Becomes the sun in the afternoon   in the evening
And in the night   and to resemble God
Is to resemble light   the way a bed
Resembles sunlight   when sunlight is spread

Across it   to resemble God is to
Remain the bed as the light slides away
The hastily assembled angel when
Humans appeared on Earth   at first the angel

Didn't see   any resemblance he
Saw his reflection in a pond and marked
Neither the similarities nor differ-
ences between himself and humans   their

Voices climbed a canyon to his tent
In the clouds and though they laughed and shouted
With voices like the voices of the other
Angels he never once   hoped he was being

Called   *If God had made me*   *for them* he
Shouted down hours   after the laughing pack
Had left the canyon   *I might watch them*
Instead   God merely hadn't called him back

After the other angels shoved him from
Heaven   instead the angel watched the sun until he
Began to think it was the eye of God
Even though he felt   sure God had

No eyes   no body   and no voice   with which
To call him back   instead he watched a forest
At the edge of the canyon he   watched it until
A different pack of humans cut the shortest

Fully grown tree down then he watched the tree as
The humans dragged it to their camp he watched the
Tree as the humans broke the tree apart he
Watched as the humans carved the parts of the tree in-

to gods with bodies and   glowering faces

He watched the humans as they bowed to the gods

He watched them   like a small child watching dancers

Forgetting his own body   bowing as they bow

The hastily assembled angel thinks
He must be more like God than people are
Especially because he like God can't
Choose to be less like God   he tilts his chair

Back his brown metal folding   chair on its
Back legs and lifts   first his right leg and then
His left   onto the wolf-sized rock he's using
As his desk   while the great flood floods the plains

The valleys and the forests far below him
And the mountains   eventually his mountain
Eventually his right   leg on the rock
His left crossed over at the ankles *Wanting*

To be like God he thinks must be the wrong way
To be like God   who doesn't want to be
Like anything   but I don't want
To be like God he heard the rising sea

First in his sleep two   nights ago he dreamed
A lion roared and couldn't stop and wept
Roaring   and in the dream the angel thought
I must record the lion's roar   and leapt

Down from his cot   in the clouds to a small village
Built like a village near a forest from
Strong trunks and supple branches   but it stood in
A desert   and the roofs were thatched with bones

The angel saw no lion there but heard
Its roar and saw   the roaring wind on the weeping
Sand   and the weeping sand in the twisting wind
And woke on the mountain woke   in falling snow like weeping

Sand   not knowing how he had gotten there   in snow and
Warm rain he woke and turned his face away
From the sun and saw instead the warm rain tearing
Snow from the mountainside he turned   his face and saw

Already he was lost inside
God's plan for the world   again he hadn't seen
In the millennia that must have led
To this   moment the workings of the plan

He slapped the ground and stood   he staggered to
His folding chair miraculously there
Folded and propped against the wolf-sized rock
And listened to the weeping and the roaring

World below him not   life but the world
Itself   thinking   This isn't   like any other
Sound   as the storm stripped   comparison from the Earth
But the angel kept the wolf in the rock

THE HASTILY ASSEMBLED ANGEL

ON CARE AND VITALITY

The hastily assembled angel watches
From the air he watches   from that point in the air
Where years from now the apex of the pyra-
mid he is watching being   built will be
Invisibly   he watches as slaves roll
Huge stones from the quarry to the pyramid the
Slave who invented   the method for moving
The stones is dead   the stones   that were too big
For human beings to move   the angel saw
The slave was killed for   attempting to correct
The implementation of his method   which
The Egyptian engineers had not at first
Completely understood   though even as
His dark blood made the dirt beside them dark
They saw the first board buckle   beneath the weight
Of the first stone   fortunately the slave had
Explained his method often to his fellow
Slaves   and they could when they were ordered to
Silently make it work the angel sees the
Slaves serve their masters most   efficiently
When they aren't talking to each other   but
They serve their masters most   quickly just after
They have devised a plan to kill their masters

THE HASTILY ASSEMBLED ANGEL

CONSIDERS HIS OWN FOREKNOWING

The hastily assembled angel wandered
The desert hidden in   a pillar of
Cloud in the day   and in a pillar of
Fire in the night   and as he wandered he
Asked himself whether   sometimes as he wandered
He asked himself   whether he really could
Be said to wander   since he after all
Could see through time   which was even better for
Seeing where he was going than seeing   through space

In the day he was a darkness in the cloud
Like rain   and in the night he was a darkness
In the fire   like God   and day and night he wondered
Why he had been given gifts even God
Hadn't been given or no even God   hadn't
Given Themselves or no no even   God did-
n't have and who he wondered ever could
Give God a gift   except he knew he was
Allowed to see through time because he was
Not God   and could be wrong   and saw through time
With many-chambered eyes   all things that might be
And God would see   only the one thing that would

Is that the one gift   he wondered   *That free beings*
Give God uncertainty   he wondered in
The cloud as the crowd followed him or followed
The darkness in the pillar   though it was
The only flaw in the pillar they could see

THE HASTILY ASSEMBLED ANGEL

MEETS THE GOD OF HUMAN FREEDOM

.

The hastily assembled angel followed
The humans to their freedom   Just he wondered like
The eyes of the angels   when they followed
Me   after the angels shoved

Me out of Heaven the   angel followed them until
They came upon a desert-colored city
Surrounded by a wall of crumbling bricks
Before which guards armed not with spears but sticks

Stood   and the humans in their freedom raised
Their fingers to their mouths   to say We have
No food   and the guards waved their empty hands
To say There is no food in the city   and

The humans in their freedom killed them both
And pounded with their bloody fists   on the splintering gates
Which shook but didn't break   the angel watched   as
The humans in their freedom made a giant calf with

A golden body   and an iron head
And slammed the calf into the gates
Which shook and broke apart   the angel saw   the
Humans in their   freedom became as hungry then

As any who had ever lived
Hungrier than the humans in the city
Who had fed   on living in a city
And the angel flew   into the burning city

And kneeled before the calf   as he had seen
So many humans kneel before the gods they
Had made   *What god is this* he wondered
I kneel before   knowing it is no god

The hastily assembled angel sits
Behind the gate and doesn't watch the gate
He watches   the expressions on the faces
Of the dozen archers posted on the gate
But only one   archer and only when
He glances   at the archer next to him
Nervously the young   archer turns his head
To glance at the older archer middle-aged
Who only looks ahead the   hastily
Assembled angel wonders who it was
Who said In the midst of life we are in death
He has heard many songs and that was one
Although he has heard none of those songs sung
Only recited   quickly as he was
Shoved off the cloud   more quickly than a human
Mind could comprehend recited as
Ten thousand other things were shouted   all at
Once by ten thousand other angels all
Of whom heard music he will never hear
He hears a   scream and he is back at the gate
Behind the gate and   what had he been doing
He wonders   as he sees a young man falling
He stands and folds his metal folding chair

The hastily assembled angel saw
One thing was like another thing and that
Thing like another everything   depend-
ed on   how high it was   the place you saw

Things from   and he had seen the Earth from where
A human couldn't see the Earth   and could-
n't tell most human things apart   and though
He hadn't ever really understood

His job he knew it had to do with seeing
And what he saw   was everything would come
Together at the same time everything
Would fall apart   and that was humans thinking

The world was meant for them and other things
Were accidental   or were decora-
tions meant for them and therefore purposeful
That humans thought that God had told them so

And what the hastily assembled angel
Thought   was that probably God had said the same thing
To every living thing   on Earth and only
Stopped when one said *Really* back   but then

Again   the hastily assembled angel
Couldn't tell human things apart   and maybe
That *Really* mattered what   would he have heard
Holy   or maybe Folly   or maybe *Kill me*

THE LONELINESS OF THE

HASTILY ASSEMBLED ANGEL

Haste makes not waste   but me or haste makes waste
And also me or haste makes waste   hello
The hastily assembled angel shouts
Down from the thunderhead at bleary Lew-

is who   just now is waking next to Clark
Who in his dream is wrestling a leaf-
Green bear and who   outside the dream is squirming
Desperately   in the dirt and leaves

Humans   *did not invent their minds the angel*
Wonders   *as he turns to watch the sunlight*
At the other end of the horizon slip
Behind the Earth *Hello   you're having fun   right*

He shouts   half to the people in the darkness
And half to the men beneath him   watching nei-
ther but the sunlight   and the dust now   swirling
Between the Earth and him the angel sees

In every speck its origin whole he sees in
One speck the skin   of the living woman it
Broke from the angel sees the skin of the dead
The many dead   in the specks now mixing with

The speck from the living woman and the specks
From trees and insects   *Nothing is alone*
He sees and says   as he has seen before   and
Now as before   his voice is hidden in thunder

And one man wakes the other   and they run

THE HASTILY ASSEMBLED ANGEL

CONSIDERS THE DUTIES OWED TO LOVE

The disappointment angel flies so close
Sometimes within a dozen feet and even   for angels
What's close on the ground is too   close in the air
So close   the hastily assembled

Angel whenever it passes by he is
Afraid   to lift his arm to wave afraid
He'll lose his arm   to the furious orbit it re-
peats   endlessly and has   it coincid-

ed the beginning of its flight   with the
Beginning of the hastily assem-
bled angel's loneliness and fascination
With human beings   which itself began

Centuries after they began to thrive   the
Beginning of his loneliness and fascination   made
A *ping* in Heaven   like the *ping* a sonar
Scanner makes as the array sends sound

Waves through the living and the dead   to map
A path through them   or launch
Explosives toward them the disappointment
Angel has orbited   since it was pushed

From Heaven   as the hastily assembled
Angel had been pushed   though the other angels had
More hurriedly   less carefully   constructed it
Teaching it only how

To scream   and so it learned to fly by falling
It learned to fly near   to the Earth
By falling to the Earth   as terror taught
It how to fly   the hastily assembled angel

From the first time he saw it knew   it was made for him
It knows I love it   even if I don't wave
He thinks   I'm sure   because it won't stop
Screaming   because it would   tear off my arm

THE HASTILY ASSEMBLED ANGEL CONSIDERS

THE LIVES OF DOGS AND OF PEOPLE

The hastily assembled angel wanders
And has   wandered through centuries of cities
And countries and millennia of cities
And countries and of women and of men   there's

No hurry now though he was hurriedly
Once brought to being   and bears the scars of that
Though slowly   in the Earth   though slowly he
Eventually began to wonder what

The hurry had been for   and if he could
Have been a better angel or have done
Better the job he did if once
They'd made him the   other angels had allowed

Him to meet God   for he has been uncertain
As people are uncertain he has nev-
er been as certain   as dogs are   who sniff
The wind that moves the curtain   and see behind the curtain

2. VARIATIONS ON

JIM LIMBER GOES TO HEAVEN

If you want to die you will have to pay for it.

—Louis MacNeice

Nobody knows I know   what happened to
Me   after I was taken from the Da-
vises some think the Yankee soldiers who
Took me I fought them hard took   me away

Some think they must have drowned me in a river
Some think they must have taken me up north
I could have disappeared in the north   forever
Easy as I could have disappeared in death

I disappeared forever and I did-
n't die   I died and disappeared forev-
er either way   I disappeared   I died
'Less you them soldiers don't   matter what you believe
It only ever matters who
Believes   and what they have the power to do

White Yankees think they're Heaven   'cause they think
They know how I was treated in the south   'cause
They know how they would treat me if they could

'Cause it ain't nothing special makes white Yan-
kees different from the white   folks down south just
Up north before the war   the loudest white folks yelled

To *save* the union   that ain't nothing
Special   I yelled when Yankees took me from
Momma Varina   she   just stretched her arms
Toward me like she   was too weak   to fight the

Yankees I was kicking them and shouting
Like they was stealing me from home   but home's
Where the white folks who take you   take you   home
Follows your sorrow   so it is like Heaven

What was it like it wasn't like the candle
Went out in my   bedroom and next I found my-
self in the sun outside I felt myself
My body   more so much I couldn't tell
For sure if it was mine I thought I was
Chasing a big dog through the tallest grass
I'd ever seen grass taller than
The tall grass me and momma hid from the master in
The night before the morning Mrs. Davis
Took me away   and somehow that dog stayed just
An inch or two ahead
I was already dead
And had been dead some time   then all at once   I saw the grass
Was giant wings it was angels' wings   whipping my hands and face

JIM LIMBER REFUSES TO ENTER HEAVEN

UNTIL HE HAS LIVED A HAPPY LIFE

I got to Heaven and I won't believe it
'Cause nobody in Heaven's gonna make
A fool of me   I told them *Send me back*
If you're good angels like they got in Heaven
I told them   *Send me back and I'll*
Believe you when I wake up   *in good boots*
Since I never *had* good boots   I'm wait-
ing on those good boots still   I'm waiting still

For them to send me back I'm waiting   to wake up   I told
Them   and at first they smiled
And said it slower like I hadn't heard
But now they just don't talk to me   I'm standing
Outside the gates and shouting *I ain't fooled*
If I've earned my reward   where is the life where I can spend it

JIM LIMBER ENTERS THE JOINT

ECONOMY OF HEAVEN AND EARTH

Well I'm in Heaven now I reckon this
Is Heaven   what will I do   how will I live
I reckon this is Heaven and I'm alive
First   I suppose I got to find a house

First I suppose I got to find some land
To work first first   before I think about
A house I got   I reckon what I got
To do first   I suppose I got to find

A man who owns a farm and needs some help
More than the help he has   I reckon all
White folks got to do is die and wait

I reckon help   comes to them every day
Since they're in Heaven   and black folks die   I reckon money
I'll never see is waiting on me

JIM LIMBER ON THE INABILITY OF

THE ENSLAVED TO SEE THEMSELVES

I always thought in Heaven I would be
An angel   I *might* be   but I don't think
I am   I didn't think I'd still be me
I guess I thought   I would be white a pink
Face floating over a white sheet   I ain't
Pictured no body under that white sheet
But that was where my body would have been
I guess I saw my pink   hands poking out
Of the parts of the sheet   where my pink arms
Would go I guess   I saw me holding my
Arms out   like I was being crucified
Except I wasn't I was   praising some-
body and floating in my whiteness like an angel

Will I still be my body if it changes

What if it Heaven was like my momma said it
Would be like gardens spread like blankets spread
Wide between rivers gardens full like rivers with good
Food all kinds fish but also okra fried hot
And bread and chicken and even candy
All served on dishes like the dishes white
Folks got what   if it Heaven was like what
We laughed about over supper sometimes   and we
Were here together now in Heaven and we saw it
Together   me and momma now
In Heaven on a picnic between those rivers
What if in Heaven we could have white things

And not be white   how would we know
How good it was if it was good for everyone

Heaven's got a long train running 'round it rides
A circuit 'round it I've been told   that cir-
cuit is a perfect circle but inside
The circle's bigger than outside   the cir-
cle I've been told   it grows inside but out-
side stays the same   it's bigger every day
But it don't never change   the long train's got
Soft seats   wide windows and the windows they
Are always as wide   as they need to be
For folks to see whatever they happen to
Be looking at they widen silently
And narrow silently   I reckon though
They widen more   as the inside circle fills   with the dead
They widen and they widen and

JIM LIMBER SEES PEOPLE

GET THE HEAVEN THEY WANT

Heaven is full of white   folks but they got
These glasses on that they don't know they're glass-
es they don't know they're wearing   but it's not
Glasses 'cause it's a wide   black blindfold 'cause
It wraps around their heads it's thick and covers
Their ears   and it ain't glasses 'cause they can't
See through it 'cept I know they see   forever
Felt like forever I   watched for my chance

I got it when a white boy fell asleep
In the cafeteria   I tiptoed o-
ver and I took his glasses I just slipped
Them on   my head even though
They were too small   I looked   and saw the white boy
Looked at my hands   but I had disappeared I saw   the white boy

I thought I was   when momma was   my momma
Who ran   was beating me and my
Momma   Varina stopped her   then she momma
Varina she looked   mad she looked me in the eye

And told me she was taking me with her
To her big house   I thought I was in Heaven
Then 'cause she stopped my pain and 'cause she scared
Me   like the angels scare   new folks in Heaven

Standing like white boys standing at the edge of
Town staring at you and they look like
Giants   but they can't be much   older
Than you   just staring at you like you look like

Nothing they ever seen   and their worst en-
emy together and they know   what they protect protects them
Heaven   ain't plenty   and it ain't protection
Heaven is when they kill you in their homes

OLD TIMES THERE

Amen, I tell you, unless you turn back and become as children,
you most certainly may not enter into the Kingdom of the heavens.

—Matthew 18:3

CHARACTERS

Jim Limber, *a mixed-race man who appears to be in his early 60s*
Jefferson Davis, *former President of the Confederate States of America—*
   he remains offstage for the duration of the play

The stage is bare and starkly lit, and the background is an almost metallic, early twilight blue. Jim Limber emerges stage right. He is wearing brown shoes, faded brown slacks, with suspenders, and a white button-up shirt, open at the collar, under which is a white T-shirt. Jim walks to the center of the stage, then turns to face the audience.

Jim Limber: We sleep.   I bet you didn't know folks sleep
   In Heaven,   but we do. I'm   sleeping now.
   Folks sleep   in Hell too. Bet you didn't know.
   Enough to keep them fresh.   Enough to keep
   Them feeling   something.   Soon as one goes numb—a
   Sinner goes numb—the   Devil loses his
   Moral authority.   They sleep,   but it's
   Always a restless sleep. It's always someone,

Some demon, chasing them,   or it's some demon,

Except the demon   has the face of their

Worst enemy or their best friend,   and when

The demon catches them, that demon stares

Them right in the eye and it   don't   say   a thing.

In Heaven, we watch their dreams,   and I have seen them

Beg for words from their worst enemies

More desperately   than I have ever seen

Them beg for words from their best friends.

(He hears a voice offstage left, and turns his head to listen.)

Jefferson Davis: *Please help*

me, Varina!   Save me! Wife! Speak to me!

Please speak to me.   If you won't speak to me,

then turn your face away, at least, or change

your expression, at least—please, Varina.

Look through me like you used to do,   so that

I feel myself encompassed by your look,

along with the whole world behind me, as

if you would hold the world behind me to

keep me before you. I don't see that look

in your face. Save me from the look I see.

JL (He turns again to face the audience. As he speaks, he glances toward the voice, then back to the audience.):

He's dreaming—Mr.   Davis. Jefferson

44

Davis,   my daddy, or he was.   I said
He was, after the Yankees took me,   when
Anyone up north asked.   And I was proud
To say so,   even though I knew he wouldn't
Have said I was his son. He's   dreaming, and
I see his dream.

JD: *Varina, look   behind*
     you. Won't you listen, at least, if you won't
     speak?   Look—it's Jim, our little Jim. He's changed
     some. He's big now.   But I know him. Jim!   Jim!

JL (visibly shaken, glancing toward the voice again, then back
to the audience):
     We . . .   uh . . .   In Heaven,   our dreams are like our
          dreams were
     On Earth,   except they're never bad.   On Earth,
     I dreamed once   I was president of the north,
     Stuck in the war forever,   and I knew somehow,
     To end the war I had to let myself
     Get shot in the head.

JD: *Jim!   You hear me, Jim.*
     It's been   such a long time. I'm somewhere, now,
     and Mrs. Davis won't respond to me.
     Though earlier she seemed to have something
     important to tell me, and chased me here,

now she stands before me like a nigger

before a plow.   Surely you can get her

talking—you were her special favorite.

Do you remember how she petted you?

JL: (He turns to face the voice.) I . . . Can you see me, Mr.
Davis?

JD: Of

course I see you, boy, though I see also

some void between us. I've long been somewhere

without even a void to contemplate.

I find myself   immobile in hard space

each day, and am freed each night only to

discover a fear of Mrs. Davis,

and run from her until she interrupts

my running, and then stands as you see now

silently before me, wearing a look

in which I do not recognize myself.

JL: I've watched you   in the observatory. I even—
Once I was watching you   run and you turned
Your head—I thought to check if Mrs. Davis
Was still   chasing you—but you didn't turn
It all the way, but just enough to see
Me.   And I thought you saw me,   but I saw your
Eyes and there wasn't nothing in them.   I
Thought if you saw me, I would see me.

JD: I
thought   I was alone. Though I hear moaning
every day,   I do not see its source, and
I have come to believe I am its source.
Mrs. Davis is here at night, but she
doesn't speak. And I have never seen you.
Where are we?

JL: Dead.   I'm dead, and so are you.
You know you're dead,   right? Don't you know you're
    dead?
You've been dead long enough   to know. I know
They . . . Where you are, they . . .   It sure don't feel good
To say it, Mr. Davis—used to feel
Good to imagine it, before I saw
You there, but . . .   Mr. Davis, you're in Hell.
And sometimes they don't like to tell folks so—
They like to let them think they're still alive.
But most folks figure it   out after ten
Years or so, maybe fifteen for some.   You've
Been dead a   hundred-twenty years—I've been
Watching you run   ninety of those years.
But never like this, in   my own dream. (He reaches
    toward the voice.) And there's
Supposed to be a barrier,   a veil,
Between us   you can't see through. How . . .

JD: Stop.   Stop!
   (Jim lowers his arm.)
   I don't . . . I do not understand what you're
   saying to me, nor why you would be so
   insulting, and cruel, as to say it.
   I know   I cannot be where you say I
   am   because Varina is here with me.

JL: That thing? That ain't   her. She's   in that place, too, but
      Not with you. That's   a demon there, with you.   It
      Wears a mask.   Mrs. Davis . . . I don't like
      To think about her.   She runs till she wakes.
      She sees you and she runs. I   had to stop
      Watching her.   She don't rest.

JD: No. This is a
   prison, and it is treachery.   I led
   my people   according to the laws of
   the nation, and according to the laws
   of God. Of God! You can't imprison me
   for doing what the law   required me to
   do.   I served the cause of freedom.

JL: Mr.
      Davis,   who do you think I am?

JD: You're   my
    jailor.   A demon!

JL: No.   I'm me.   I'm Jim.

JD: How can you be Jim?   Where is your demon?

JL: I'm free,   in Heaven.   I've been here ninety years.
    After the war, you   didn't look for me,
    Did you? I grew up up   north.   Wasn't free,
    Though—not till I saw you.   When I got here
    I looked for you. I looked and then I asked.
    But none of the   angels would say.   But then
    I found the observatory,   saw your dreams.
    You pleading with that demon in that mask—
    I saw you   and I felt ashamed.   But I
    Saw you.   That demon has you like you had
    Me—pleading with a mask I put on you—
    The year I lived with you.   And all my life
    I only wanted one more chance to plead
    With you—with the mask.   But I don't want that now.

JD: You always were a loyal boy.   You fought
    like a tiger when the Yankees took you.

JL: I was an old man   when I died. I wasn't
    Old   like you got to be, but I was ready.

49

I might have died   differently, if I could have

Chosen how—but I was old enough not

To care to choose.   I died an old man,   woke

Up an old man in Heaven.   And the first thing

I did, I looked for you,   I asked the an-

gels where you were.

JD: *Be loyal now. Help me.*

JL: White folks get old—a rich man, like you were,

Gets old, he finds a seat   in a booth waiting

For him,   and all he has to do is sit him-

self   down and it's *his* show playing   down there

On a stage other white folks laid across

The backs of all us Negroes.   I'm old soon

As I can't hold the stage   up—I'm old soon

As I get crushed.   I died, and then I was

Old.

JD: *Enough, Jim!   Look—she turns away from*

me.

JL: But I wasn't never once a child,

Except the year I lived   with you and Mrs.

Davis—I always was   a man or 'bout

To be, before and since. So,   when I got

To Heaven, I looked for you and Mrs. Davis—

JD: I think she will leave me, Jim.   Please help me.

JL: I thought, *What's   Heaven if I ain't a child?*

JD: Please.   Help me!   I'm in prison.   A spy has
      taken me,   and I am bound so tightly
      sometimes I feel I am submerged in stone.
      But I find freedom in my dreams.   Help me
      find some comfort, too.   Jim?   For old times' sake?

Jim takes a step toward the voice, pauses, thinking, for a few
seconds, then continues off the stage.

LIMBO

Such as I've been I am I never was
Bad or a good boy   'cept as I was born
Bad like you know the badness in a glass
Of fresh milk if   you leave it in the sun

Will be exposed by the blazing inquiry
Bad like the sun won't make it   fresher not
Bad like a white boy's badness lights the sky
With a strange second sun that dies   unnat-

urally from the sky   that while it shines
Down on him makes the ground he walks a stage
And when it dies he is himself again
A living Negro never walked a stage

We are the ghosts of who comes   after us
And their memorial I   bet I was sent
To Limbo   'cause whoever watches was-
n't sure what good and bad things I had done

But saw the good and bad   things millions of
Negroes had done before me on my back
And couldn't add the figures up   and thought
Limbo was good enough and not to dark-

en Heaven   darker than Heaven has to be
Or it might be a storm   of Negroes in
Heaven I bet whoever watches sees
A storm of Negroes piled high thrashing on

My back whoever watches sees a pile
Of Negroes thinks   they're thrashing 'cause it's so
Many in one place but the thrashing's all
The rush of the eye from one black body to

The next and it's no   thrashing in the bod-
ies but the wrong is in the eye   I bet
Whoever watches didn't see I had
A storm of Negroes on my back but it

Was a black cloud like the black clouds I've seen
In the far Heaven I've seen from Limbo   like
The clouds I've seen   from which I've seen stars born
Such storms as are the glory of the dark

2. VARIATIONS ON

JIM LIMBER GOES TO HEAVEN

If you want to die you will have to pay for it.

—Louis MacNeice

The gates ain't gates   it's dreams   but memories
Like dreams the gates of Heaven memories good
Memories and good memories with bad
Parts but the bad parts   have been cleared away

And in the spaces where they were
It's nothing   there but light white light but al-
so orange light   green light and blue light fall-
ing waterfall blue light   but also there

It's nothing there the spaces where   the bad parts
Were they're the spaces in-
Between the bars   the good times are the bars

And folks get stuck outside the gates consider-
ing just how good their good times were   if you want in
Make yourself small   squeeze like a child   through the
    light between the bars

JIM LIMBER ON THE PEACE WHICH

PASSETH ALL UNDERSTANDING

First thing I saw that heartened me in Heaven
Was a dead field first   thing beyond the gates
I might have thought if I had seen when I
Was still alive a field in such a state
I might have wondered whether   it had ever
Been cultivated whether Negroes had
Worked it and if I had I might have wondered
How many died before it got so bad
How many Negroes did it take for the field
To die   the deaths of Negroes being the life
And death of the Earth   I might have asked the dirt
I might have asked the limp brown grass   but there was noth-
ing   human in the field   I had never seen that
Before   death with no people in it

1.

I still don't know if Jesus was the dog or Jesus

See Jesus   doesn't make himself

Apparent like I might have thought he would've   if

I'd ever thought about it but I guess   I just thought he was

Most of the time   smiling and judging on

His throne   and maybe sometimes he'd hop   up   and jog

A few circles around God   the father like a dog

Chasing its tail   then sit back down

Grinning like it's a joke between them

Or something maybe I just thought

He sometimes   probably he's got

To be a man still   even

In Heaven even though the other men

In Heaven are dead   so I get to Heaven and

First thing I see first living thing I see
After the gate just past the field just past
The gate it's two things it's
A tall white man in a white robe   who looks like Je-
sus in a painting in a Bible made for children
Smiling and waving next   to him   facing him there's
This dog   looks like it was about to be a Ger-
man shepherd but some bloodhound fell in
Its path looks   like a floppy wolf
And it doesn't   care for the man it's got its back up
Its head   down and it's growling like it's
Fixing to kill him   but like it's   scared the man will

Kill it if it doesn't   kill him first the way
A growling dog can seem to want to cry

And the man doesn't seem to notice it

I notice I   hear the dog growling from

The middle of the field   but the man doesn't seem

To notice anything in Heaven but

Me   and I stop a good ten feet away

From him   from the man and the dog   from both

But mostly from the dog   whose teeth

Are white as clouds   whose fur is gray

As rain in clouds   who looks like a day thinking

I stop   and the man speaks to me   he says I *see*

In your eyes a dog   *still stands next to me*

I see the dog   *still bares its teeth the dog is speaking*

Through you   but also you   sustain the dog it doesn't know

You have this pow-

4 .

er you   with your silence and fear

You feed the dog   step   forward friend   and tell me who I am

Come   speak my name

My name   will drive the dog away almost   before

He says the   eh in away the

Dog bites his thigh at first I think the dog has

Bitten clean through the meat   but then I see its   tongue is

Bleeding I see the man is dissipating

Like fog   and the dog turns and runs

Deep into Heaven   and disappears so fast I couldn't have

Even if I had wanted to   chased it through Heav-

en when   I turn to the man again the man is gone

I run to where he stood

From the empty air   blood drips into the pool of blood

I heard folks growing up the older slaves
Talking about   the fields of bliss   in the fields
I guess these are the fields of bliss   and heav-
enly reward   these fields of dead   the old-
er   and I never thought about this when
I was alive but   the older you get
In Heaven the   older you get   it ain't
Bodies in Heaven but your mind you got

Beautiful youngsters everywhere   and you
Would never know until they talk ain't nothing
About them young   except the dew and dew-
y fields   wither in dew   as often
As they are green in it   and you think they ain't smiling
They get to keep their bodies   and their minds die

JIM LIMBER IN HEAVEN

WRITES HIS NAME IN WATER

You walk through Heaven anywhere to any-
where on that soft green grass   or nowhere it
Don't matter anywhere you walk a bright
And cool and it's about   a foot wide stream of
The cleanest water anywhere with each
Step you take parts the grass beside you
On your left side   if you're left-handed
And on your right side otherwise   just reach

Down if you're thirsty or you're dirty or
You're hot   they got the sun in Heaven still
And folks get hot sometimes   me   sometimes I
Walk just to see the stream appear
Sometimes I lead it   through my name   on Earth I couldn't spell
My name   now my great thirst has been revealed to me

HEAVEN IN HEAVEN

I see visions   in my head of Heaven
I see what I'm pretty sure is Heaven
Even in Heaven   Heaven is a garden
Not Eden   but an ordinary garden
Just like the garden Missus kept I wasn't
Allowed to enjoy that garden   but I wasn't
Old enough then to do as I was told
Always or worry always   momma told
Me on the road when we were running we were
Running so Master wouldn't whip me   we were
Running 'cause I had strayed   into the garden
One time too many   and had spoiled the garden
For Missus and for Master Heaven
Looks like that garden   but it is set free in Heaven

Never was good with women   I mean I
Had a few woman friends   at the factory
But that was work   and sometimes I think they
Were nice to me because they had to be

Nice to the men   even the men beneath them
And I retired where I started   down
But nobody   has to be nice in Heaven
Nobody has to smile   God is a wom-

an for some folks   in Heaven and
God is a man for others and for some
Folks God is both and neither one   for some folks God
Is neither one and nothing in-between

I see folks'   Gods whenever I see their faces
But God don't look like anybody here
For me   God is a woman   and Her face is
Black as a bright black stone   I've walked with Her

On the path between the apple orchard
And the garden   in spring   when the orchard is a garden

I ride the train for nothing sometimes just
Because I can   because I couldn't once
But I don't know if I'm supposed to count
That   if this life is more of what life was

Or something new   I never suffered on the train I ride
But I ain't suffered at the hands of
Every white man I met and I still under-
stood who was white and who was something white

And altogether black at the same time
It wasn't nothing in the man or me but some-
thing in the life we shared

But I mean *share* like prisoners
Share loneliness   I ride the train now like I never suf-
fered on a train   sometimes I never suffered in my life

Heaven's a horse a train a ship with no
Captain or with a captain but the captain is
A Negro   or a rowboat tied but loose-
ly to   the dock the river peaceful no-
body or everybody is   a Ne-
gro it's a hundred Negroes on the dock
A thousand Negroes like when Jesus broke
The bread to feed ten   thousand peo-
ple maybe fifteen and the bread just grew
And grew the dock just grows and grows beneath them
Ten thousand Negroes cheering you to freedom
A hundred thousand and you got good shoes
And walk to the rowboat smiling and untie it
But Heaven ain't you running but you staying

What if I had been born in Heaven do
They do that here   I've never seen a baby
But I see full-grown people who
I hear the angels whispering   they say they
Were babies when they died   I always look
Those people in the eye   but I don't think
They see me   and I've never heard them speak
They just walk around in sailor hats with blank
Looks on their faces   those white hats with the blue
Anchors   I sometimes see them walking
With their mouths open the first one I saw
I saw like that   and when I tried to talk to
Him it was like I wasn't there
So   I peeked   in his mouth

and in his mouth was the whole sky and stars

I. FRESH EYES FOR A FRESH WORLD

The hastily assembled angel climbed
The ladder God had many times proposed
The prophets build the prophets   never built it
The ladder to the sky   and Heaven in the sky
The prophets never built it   knowing God

Was testing them   but also teasing them
Since all God's tests are two tests one   for the Father
And one for the Son   and nothing for the Holy
Spirit who broods   over them like a meddlesome
Neighbor   watching two young brothers play

Switch on a stoop from the second floor across
The street   whose mother never would have let
Him he reminds himself   take an expensive
Toy like that outside   if he had owned such toys
Ever as the Nintendo Switch and prophets

The angel built the ladder   first one rung
And then another   all the way to Heaven
Then flew back down to the bottom   since he wanted
To climb it properly   then started up again
Now I will tell the rungs as the angel saw them

For whom for who could say   each rung was like
A thousand rungs the first rung who could say
How many feet from the ground it was how many
Miles from the ground more   than the higher rungs it looked
Like most rungs on most ladders made by humans

And to the angel looked most like a rung on
A fire escape   and was the rung if any
Of the rungs were visible to humans a
Human most likely would have spotted *Maybe   someone
Is watching me right now* the angel won-

dered as he stepped   to the second rung   *But all she
Sees is a single foot   my lower foot
Rising and disappearing in the stars*
Though as the angel climbed he pictured himself falling
Though he could fly   and so could only stare

Straight ahead at the rungs   the first   was nar-
row only as   wide as two human feet
Of average width   and painted black the paint had
Bubbled and flaked away in spots exposing fire-
Red and clay-red   patches of rust   that swirled

Beneath the paint like blood   tumbling through
A vein   the second rung   was wider and

Rectangular and made of glass and filled with
Water and tiny plastic animal figures two
Of every kind of animal all brightly

Colored some   yellow some blue some green
Some pink   vibrations from the angel's step
Shook them to life   the third rung was a sky-
Blue thread strung not   in the middle of the gap between
The rung below it and the rung above it

But just above   the middle just above
Enough for any lifted foot to miss
It and come down on nothingness the angel
Had as he strung it called this rung The Rung   of the Love
Of Human Beings and even when he found

It his bare foot was cut by it and bled
The fourth rung was a row of puffed white rice
Kernels implanted in a strip of moist
Chewed gum   to look like teeth in gums   the angel had
Whistled and giggled as he made this rung

But now he grimaced as he stepped from The Rung of
The Love of Human Beings   to the rung of soggy
Crumbling teeth These   teeth my God he thought
These disgusting   soggy teeth how   could a loving
God have allowed these   teeth to exist   and mid-

way through the thought   the angel reached the fifth
Rung the fifth rung   was locusts strung together
On a golden chain   a replica
Of the enormous golden chain that bound the Earth
To Heaven   in the days before men made

Weapons from the links   at the bottom of the chain
And God cursed gold with softness   when the angel
Stepped on the rung the locusts chirred   as if
They were alive   power   had gone from him   return-
ing them to life   though it returned to him

The moment his foot left the rung the sixth rung
Was a wide-open black   book and its pages
Flipped one by one in the wind   from the first to the last
And back to the first again   dark red ink oozed from each page
And rolled thick down the ladder to the fifth rung

Where when it touched the locusts the ink turned
The blue-green color of their blood   at the seventh
Rung the angel rested   and the rung
That had before the angel sat his full weight down
On it been nearly formless wide and lumpy

Soft   muddy even   flattened as the an-
gel settled in   and flattened and expanded

And took the imprint of the angel when he
Leaned over and closed his eyes   and when the angel leaned
Over his wings cut channels in the rung

Rivers and narrow   feathery streams the channels
Filled with the clear water   that flowed from the angel's
Pores as he dreamed   a long and violent
Dream   in the dream he dreamed   on the seventh rung the angel
In the dream slept on the rung   for hundreds of

Millions of years   and meteorites and lightning
Storms tore at the surface of the rung   and in
The dream the angel woke to wrestle with the
Pinkish   amorphous sky   he stood   girded for the fight in
A leaf-green singlet much too big for him   but

Cinched with a golden rope   and growled and his
Growl echoed through the new   valleys his body
Had made and animals big cats and lizards
Bipeds and quadrupeds   invertebrates birds fish
Appeared   in the dream and in the waking world

And growled and hissed and sang in answer to
His growl   and the sky fell on the angel then
And in his first defense   he seemed a match
For the sky rolling   on his back   when the sky fell
On him   and kicking the sky off with both

Feet using   the sky's weight and force against it
Continuing the motion of his roll he
Leapt to his feet and turned to face the sky
Then growled a winded   second growl   and heard diminished
Yelps in response   that seemed to come from far

Away   or from behind a wall he could-
n't see   the hard sky roiled before him   glancing
Up he saw an orangish pink sun
Glowing in a void   and felt no heat   and felt no cold
No summer and no winter from the sun

And no light   though it shone from the void brightly
Down   the sun shone on him and on the rung
Like any farther star   whose heat is an
Idea of heat   whose light is an idea of light the
Now fearful angel rushed at the sky   but couldn't

Grasp it he   could only feel it when it
Fell on him he   stumbled   it fell on him
Then rose and fell on him again   and then
Again he couldn't get his feet beneath him one   last
Time the sky fell on him   and he was pinned

In the dream as soon   as the angel was subdued
The sky returned to the void and filled the void

The heat and light of the sun   again poured down
Through the sky to the rung   and the animals on the rung
    with new
Strength growled and hissed and cooed and sang   to each

Other   in the dream and in the waking world
In the dream they made their noises and the angel
Listened knowing   as a dreamer knows
The animals were now   forgetting him   they could-
n't sense him anymore he knew   and he

Was happy   and in the waking world the singing
Of the animals woke him from his dream   and slowly
He opened   first one eye   and then the other
Sat up   and rubbed his eyes   then stood   and seeing his
    dream in
The life on the rung   he stepped from the rung to Heaven

ACKNOWLEDGMENTS

Thanks to Lucie Brock-Broido, Timothy Donnelly, Jonathan Galassi, Derek Gromadzki, Susan Howe, Anastasios Karnazes, Dorothea Lasky, Deborah Paredez, Taylor Supplee, and G. C. Waldrep for their friendship, support, and advice during the writing of this book. Thank you to Melissa McCrae, Sylvia Teters-McCrae, Nicholas McCrae, and Eden McCrae for making my life possible. And thanks to the editors and staffs of the following journals, in which earlier versions of these poems first appeared:

The American Poetry Review: "The Ladder to Heaven"

At Length: "Old Times There"

The Baffler: "The Hastily Assembled Angel on Care and Vitality"

Crazyhorse: "Jim Limber on the Gates of Heaven," "Jim Limber Tells the Truth About His Fate," and "Jim Limber's Home Is No Earthly Home"

Hyperallergic: "Jim Limber on the Gardens of the Face of God"

The Kenyon Review: "Jim Limber in Heaven Writes His Name in Water"

Magma: "Jim Limber on the Inability of the Enslaved to See Themselves" and "The Loneliness of the Hastily Assembled Angel"

Michigan Quarterly Review: "The Hastily Assembled Angel at the Gate"

The New Yorker: "Jim Limber in Heaven Is a Nexus at Which the Many Heavens of the Multiverse Converge," "Jim Limber on Continuity in Heaven," "Jim Limber on the Peace Which Passeth All Understanding," "Jim Limber on the White Embrace," and "Jim Limber's Theodicy"

Poetry: "The Hastily Assembled Angel Falls at the Beginning of the World," "The Hastily Assembled Angel Considers the Lives of Dogs and of People," and "The Wings of the Hastily Assembled Angel"

Virginia Quarterly Review: "Heaven in Heaven," "Jesus and the Mongrel Dog," and "Jim Limber Refuses to Enter Heaven Until He Has Lived a Happy Life"

The Yale Review: "The Hastily Assembled Angel on Care and Vitality" and "Jim Limber Burning Where No Fire Is"

"Jim Limber Sees People Get the Heaven They Want" was originally published in *How We Fight White Supremacy: A Field Guide to Black Resistance*, edited by Akiba Solomon and Kenrya Rankin.

"The Tree of Knowledge" was originally published as part of the Academy of American Poets' Poem-A-Day project.

"The Hastily Assembled Angel at the Gate" was republished by *Poetry Daily*.

Special thanks to the John Simon Guggenheim Foundation and the Lannan Foundation for their support during the writing of this book.